.

A Note to Parents and Teachers

SAINSBURY'S READING SCHEME is a compelling reading programme for children, designed in conjunction with leading literacy experts, including Cliff Moon M.Ed. Cliff Moon has spent many years as a teacher and teacher educator specializing in reading and has written more than 160 books for children and teachers. He reviews regularly for teachers' journals.

Beautiful illustrations and superb full-colour photographs combine with engaging, easy-to-read stories to offer a fresh approach to each subject in the series. Each book in the SAINSBURY'S READING SCHEME programme is guaranteed to capture a child's interest while developing his or her reading skills, general knowledge, and love of reading.

The five levels of the programme are aimed at different reading abilities, enabling you to choose the books that are exactly right for your child:

Yellow Level – Learning to read
Green Level – Beginning to read
Gold Level – Beginning to read alone
Ruby Level – Reading alone
Sapphire Level – Proficient readers

The "normal" age at which a child begins to read can be anywhere from three to eight years old. Adult participation through the lower levels is very helpful for providing encouragement, discussing storylines and sounding out unfamiliar words.

No matter which level you select, you can be sure that you are helping your child learn to read, then read to learn!

LONDON, NEW YORK, MUNICH,
MELBOURNE, AND DELHI

Project Editor Deborah Murrell
Art Editor Catherine Goldsmith
Senior Art Editor Clare Shedden
Managing Editor Bridget Gibbs
Senior DTP Designer
Bridget Roseberry
Production Shivani Pandey
Picture Librarian Diane Legrande
Picture Researcher Marie Osborn
Jacket Designer Karen Burgess
Natural History Consultant
Theresa Greenaway

Reading Consultant
Cliff Moon M.Ed.

This edition published in 2014
First published in Great Britain by
Dorling Kindersley Limited
80 Strand, London WC2 0RL
A Penguin Random House Company

001-273588-Sept/2014

**A CIP catalogue record for this book is
available from the British Library.**

ISBN 978-0-7513-1472-4

Colour reproduction by Colourscan, Singapore
Printed and bound in China by L. Rex Printing Co., Ltd.

The publisher would like to thank the following for their
kind permission to reproduce their photographs:

Key: t=top, b=bottom, l=left, r=right, c=centre
Bruce Coleman Ltd: Dr. P. Evans 10-11. **Gables:** 4-5, 14-15, 20-21.
Robert Harding Picture Library: 8-9. **N.H.P.A.:** Martin Harvey 23.
Oxford Scientific Films: Edwin Sadd 24-25; Gerald Thompson 13;
Konrad Wothe 30-31; Michael Fogden 22l; Richard Packwood 6-7.
Planet Earth Pictures: M & C Denis-Huot Front Jacket; Thomas
Dressor Front Jacket; Jonathan P. Scott 21r. **Ian Redmond:** 18-19.

All other images © Dorling Kindersley.
For further information see: www.dkimages.com

Discover more at
www.dk.com

Sainsbury's
Reading Scheme

Green Level
Beginning to read

Feeding Time

Written by Lee Davis

It is morning and
the sun is rising.
Animals that eat in the daytime
start to look for food.

A gorilla yawns in his nest.
He reaches out his hairy hand
to feel for a tasty plant.
He has breakfast in bed!

The elephants are ready
for breakfast, too.
They wrap their trunks
around clumps of grass.

They curl their trunks
to break off the grass and then
put it into their mouths.

Another elephant snaps off
branches from a big tree.
He chews the bark
on each branch.

bark

A large elephant knows
there are some crunchy seed pods
in the tall trees.
He stretches out his trunk
to reach them.

seed pods

Zebras reach down
to nibble the grass.

They bite the grass
with their front teeth.

A giraffe can reach the tree tops
with her long neck.
She wraps her tongue around
the tasty, tender shoots and
tears the shoots
off the branches.

shoots

The elephants wander
through the forest until
they find some banana plants.
They shake the branches
to make the bananas fall off.

A rhino spends most of the day eating grass.

An oxpecker clings to the rhino.

The oxpecker eats ticks
and insects on the rhino's skin.
He pecks at them
with his pointed beak.

tick

A chimpanzee is looking
for termites to eat.
He digs with a stick
into a huge termite hill.
He makes a large hole
in the termite hill and
the termites spill out.

termites

Elephants need to eat salt.
They do not get enough salt
in their food so
they dig up
clumps of salt to eat.

A herd of buffalo
moves to the river
for a drink.
Crocodiles watch and wait,
lying as still as rocks.

Slowly, a crocodile
swims closer.
Maybe he can grab
a young buffalo
for his dinner.

Hippos spend the hot day
in the water.

In the evening, the air is cooler.

So they come out

to eat the short grass

on the river banks.

As the sun sets,
the elephants enjoy
a late evening snack.

Maybe some more fruit
and then a long, cool drink!

Glossary

Bark
the outer part of a tree trunk or branches

Seed pods
cases with the seeds of plants inside

Shoots
young plants that grow from a larger one

Termites
Insect that feed on wood and build mounds

Tick
a bug on the skin of an animal that sucks its blood

CERTIFICATE
of Reading

My name is

_____

I have read

_____

Date

_____